Science Matters! | Volume 14

Life cycles

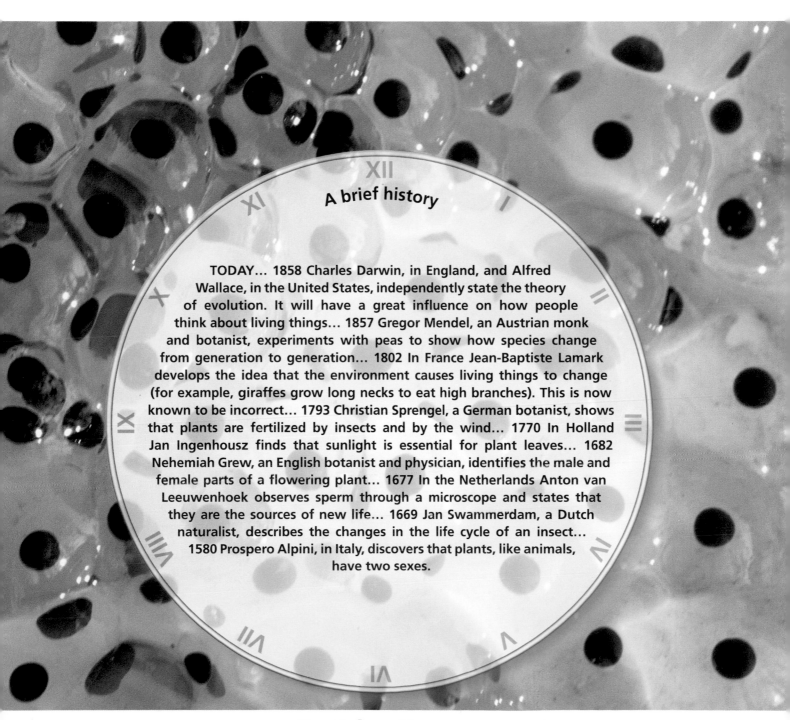

A brief history

TODAY... 1858 Charles Darwin, in England, and Alfred Wallace, in the United States, independently state the theory of evolution. It will have a great influence on how people think about living things... 1857 Gregor Mendel, an Austrian monk and botanist, experiments with peas to show how species change from generation to generation... 1802 In France Jean-Baptiste Lamark develops the idea that the environment causes living things to change (for example, giraffes grow long necks to eat high branches). This is now known to be incorrect... 1793 Christian Sprengel, a German botanist, shows that plants are fertilized by insects and by the wind... 1770 In Holland Jan Ingenhousz finds that sunlight is essential for plant leaves... 1682 Nehemiah Grew, an English botanist and physician, identifies the male and female parts of a flowering plant... 1677 In the Netherlands Anton van Leeuwenhoek observes sperm through a microscope and states that they are the sources of new life... 1669 Jan Swammerdam, a Dutch naturalist, describes the changes in the life cycle of an insect... 1580 Prospero Alpini, in Italy, discovers that plants, like animals, have two sexes.

Dr. Brian Knapp

Word list

These are some science words that you should look out for as you go through the book. They are shown using CAPITAL letters.

ANNUAL
Plants that complete their life cycle in one year.

DISPERSE
To scatter. Most plants scatter their seeds in order to have the best chance for survival.

DORMANT
A period of resting, usually so that a plant can survive harsh conditions such as a cold winter or a long drought.

EGG
A tiny cell that develops in a female animal and that contains half of the genes needed to make a new life, together with nourishment. Also an immature animal in a shell.

EXTINCT
A group of living things that has died, leaving no more to breed.

FERTILIZATION/FERTILIZE
The joining of male and female sex cells to create a complete set of instructions for a new life.

FLOWER
The part of a plant that contains the organs for reproduction. Plants that use insects for pollination often have flowers with brightly colored petals.

FRUIT
The swollen and fleshy area that develops at the bottom of a flower after fertilization. It contains the seeds.

GENE
The part of the cell that contains the instructions for a new life.

GERMINATION/GERMINATE
The process in which a seed takes in water, and its seed case breaks open to release the root.

LARVA
An early stage of the life cycle of an insect. A caterpillar is an example of a larva.

LIFE CYCLE
The series of stages in the growth of a living thing from fertilization until death.

LIFE SPAN
The length of time over which a living thing lives.

MOLT
In insects the skin that is shed from time to time in order for them to grow.

NECTAR
A sweet, sticky substance produced by flowers that attracts insects and other animals because of its food value.

NUTRITIOUS
A food that contains substance for healthy growth. The more concentrated these substances are, the more nutritious the food.

POLLINATION/POLLINATE
The transfer of pollen between the male parts of one flower and the female parts of another flower.

PUPA
The stage of the life cycle of an insect between the larva and the adult insect.

REPRODUCTION/REPRODUCE
The uniting of the male and female sex cells to create new life.

SPECIES
A particular type of living thing. All members of a species look and behave similarly.

SPERM
The male sex cell that contains half the genes needed for new life.

Contents

	Page

What is a life cycle?

During their lives all living things go through stages as they grow up, get older, and die. This is called a life cycle.

Living things all share the same pattern: they are born, they grow up, and they die. This is called a **LIFE CYCLE**.

Everything that has ever lived has had a life cycle. In some living things the life cycle can be very long. Some trees live for thousands of years. People can also have quite a long life cycle, usually about 70 years. But many living things have much shorter life cycles. Many flowering plants, for example, grow up, set seed, and die all within a few months. Some insects have a life cycle of just a few days.

Birth

In plants the life cycle often begins with the sprouting of a seed (Picture 1). In animals the life cycle begins with the hatching of an egg or the birth of young (Picture 2).

▼ (Picture 1) This is a life cycle of a plant. It shows the stages of life of a coniferous tree—the kind we often use for Christmas trees. You can think of it starting with the sprouting of new seeds (1). (There is more on plants beginning on Page 6.)

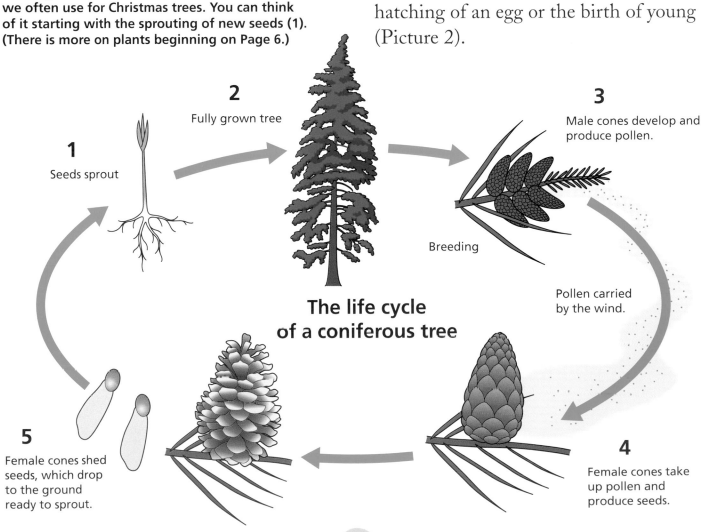

The life cycle of a coniferous tree

1 Seeds sprout

2 Fully grown tree

3 Male cones develop and produce pollen.

Breeding

Pollen carried by the wind.

4 Female cones take up pollen and produce seeds.

5 Female cones shed seeds, which drop to the ground ready to sprout.

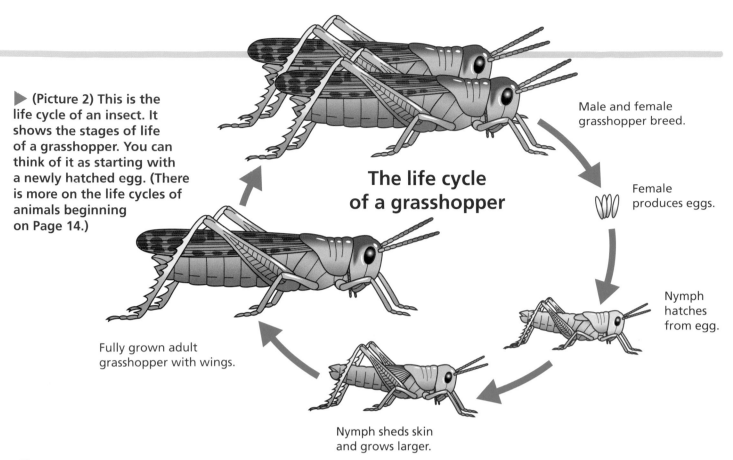

▶ (Picture 2) This is the life cycle of an insect. It shows the stages of life of a grasshopper. You can think of it as starting with a newly hatched egg. (There is more on the life cycles of animals beginning on Page 14.)

The life cycle of a grasshopper

Male and female grasshopper breed.

Female produces eggs.

Nymph hatches from egg.

Nymph sheds skin and grows larger.

Fully grown adult grasshopper with wings.

Growing up

When a living thing begins its life, it is small and weak. If it is a seedling, it can be attacked by disease, be trampled by animals, or have its shoot eaten. If it is a young animal, it may also be killed by disease, or it may be eaten by other animals for food. But if it survives these early dangers, it grows rapidly and is soon more able to defend itself.

Breeding

When they reach a certain stage, usually close to being fully grown, living things are able to breed; that is, they can now produce new living things. This is called **REPRODUCTION**. It is vital if the life cycle is to continue. At this time differences between male and female living things often become clear.

When plants and animals breed, they produce new young. Female animals often carry the new developing life until it is ready to survive on its own.

After breeding

Some plants and animals die soon after breeding. Butterflies and **ANNUAL** plants are common examples. But others survive longer and breed again. Eventually, however, all plants and animals die.

The stages in a life cycle

By linking the stages of life together in a circle, you can see how each stage relates to the others.

Summary
- There are stages in the lives of all living things.
- The stages can be linked together into a life cycle.

How seeds sprout

A seed contains a tiny plant and a supply of food. When conditions are favorable, the seed bursts open, and the plant grows out.

A plant's life cycle begins with a seed. A seed contains all the materials to make a new plant, protected by a tough, weather-resistant coat.

When a seed is released from its parent, it is almost dry. There is just enough water in the seed to keep the tiny plant alive, but there is not enough water present for the plant to grow.

The dry conditions inside the seed protect the plant and its food supply in two ways. It protects them from cold temperatures. If a water-filled seed froze, the water would expand as it turned into ice and would destroy the plant. The dry conditions also keep diseases from growing inside the seed and feeding on the tiny plant and its supply of food.

Dormancy

A seed does not sprout as soon as it leaves its parent plant. It remains inactive, or **DORMANT**, until the right time to start

▼ **(Picture 1) The sprouting of a runner bean.**

Shoot grows to find light and air

Dormant seed

Germinating seed sprouts a root

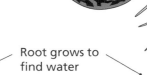

Root grows to find water

growing. For example, it may not start to grow until conditions are warm enough or the soil is moist enough.

Germination

The food stored in the seed is used by the tiny plant to give it the energy and materials it needs to begin growing. However, the seed also needs water and minerals (from the soil), oxygen (from the air), and sunlight (for energy) if it is to grow into a fully grown plant.

The seed begins by taking in water and air through a small hole in the outer coat of the seed.

As the plant grows, the first thing it needs is more water, so the first part of the plant to grow out of the seed is the root. When the seed begins to grow, and the root appears, the seed has **GERMINATED** (Pictures 1 and 2).

The seedling

With a reliable water supply from the root, the plant can grow large enough to split open its seed coat. That allows more oxygen to reach the plant. Then a shoot (which will carry the stem, leaves, and flowers) emerges from the seed. By this time the seed's energy is all but used up, so it must get new energy from sunlight. It does so by quickly sending up a stem and growing a pair of leaves. A green-colored chemical in the leaves traps sunlight and turns it into energy and food for the growing seedling.

Summary
- A seed germinates by sending out a root.
- To get the energy it needs to grow, the seed produces a stem and leaves.

▲▶ **(Picture 2) The stages of the sprouting of a chestnut tree. It is a long-lived (perennial) plant. Compare it to the short-lived (annual) runner bean, and you will see that the growth stages are just the same.**

Flowers, fruits, and seeds

When flowering plants reach the breeding stage of their life cycle, they produce flowers. They develop into fruits that contain seeds.

When a plant is fully grown, it produces **FLOWERS** (Picture 1). The male parts of the flowers contain pollen. Pollen is vital to the life cycle of the plant. It must pass from one flower to another for seeds to be made. The movement of pollen is called **POLLINATION**.

How flowers become pollinated

Flowering plants have two ways of moving their pollen. They can use animals, such as insects, or the wind (Picture 2).

Flowers that need insects are colorful and often scented. The color and the smell attract insects to them. The flower also provides the insect with a drink

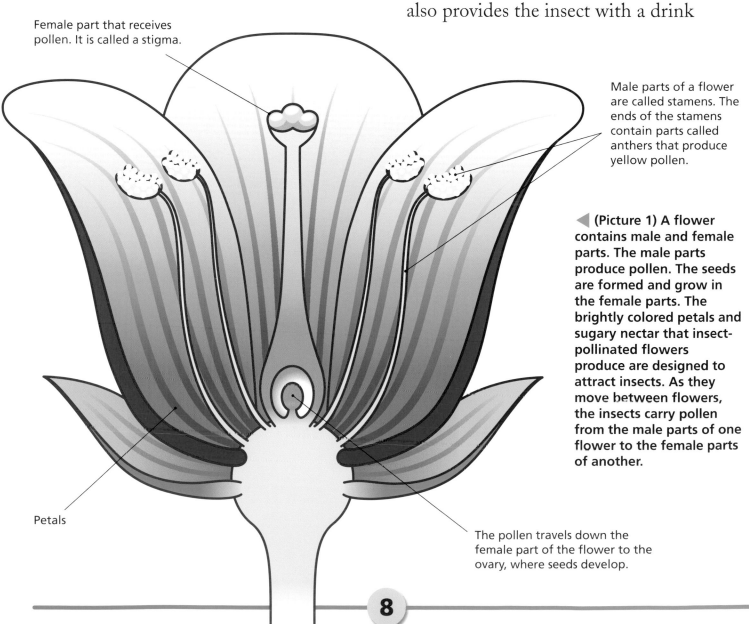

Female part that receives pollen. It is called a stigma.

Male parts of a flower are called stamens. The ends of the stamens contain parts called anthers that produce yellow pollen.

◀ (Picture 1) A flower contains male and female parts. The male parts produce pollen. The seeds are formed and grow in the female parts. The brightly colored petals and sugary nectar that insect-pollinated flowers produce are designed to attract insects. As they move between flowers, the insects carry pollen from the male parts of one flower to the female parts of another.

Petals

The pollen travels down the female part of the flower to the ovary, where seeds develop.

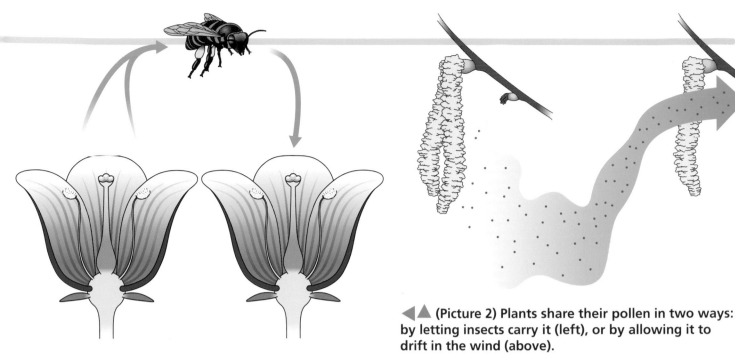

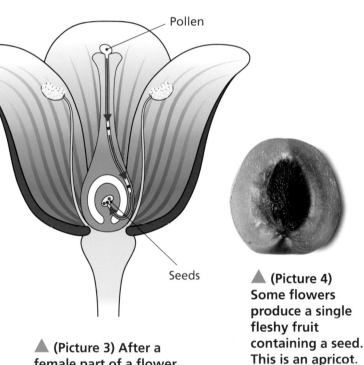

(Picture 2) Plants share their pollen in two ways: by letting insects carry it (left), or by allowing it to drift in the wind (above).

Pollen

Seeds

(Picture 3) After a female part of a flower has received pollen, it swells, and seeds develop. As the seeds grow, the petals wither.

(Picture 4) Some flowers produce a single fleshy fruit containing a seed. This is an apricot.

of sugary food called **NECTAR**. As the insects move from flower to flower in search of nectar, pollen sticks to their bodies. In this way pollen can be carried between flowers.

Insects take the pollen away to other flowers of the same kind. The male parts of a flower release their pollen before the female parts of that flower become sticky. Only flowers that have already released their pollen will have sticky pads to trap pollen carried from other flowers.

Where seeds develop

Once a flower has been pollinated, the base of the flower swells (Picture 3). This is called **FERTILIZATION**. Later, the petals may fall off, and the center of the flower may change color. Inside the swollen part of the flower—the **FRUIT**—new seeds begin to develop. A fruit is the container for the seed (Picture 4). It may be juicy like an orange, hard like a nut, or feathery like a dandelion parachute.

Summary
- A plant produces flowers when it is mature.
- There are two kinds of flowers—insect-pollinated flowers and wind-pollinated flowers.
- The fruits and seeds form in the center of the flower once it has been pollinated.

How seeds are scattered

Plants have a range of ways of spreading their seeds. They may use the wind, animals, or even water.

If seeds were not scattered, they would simply fall to the ground below the flower. When the seeds germinated, the seedlings would have to struggle with other seedlings and with their parent plant for water and minerals (Picture 1). The leaves of the seedlings would overlap, and they would all be shaded by the parent plant. Under these conditions the chances of any seedling growing well are not good.

To overcome this problem, seeds have developed ways of being carried away, or **DISPERSED**, from the parent plant. This way they have a better chance of growing into healthy plants.

Carried by the wind

Seeds have many ways of being scattered. The smallest seeds are so light that they can be carried by the wind (Picture 2).

▲ **(Picture 1)** All of these seedlings have to compete for the same water, soil nourishment, and light.

◀▶ **(Picture 2)** Many seeds use the wind, from the microscopic spores that leave the underside of a mushroom (right), to the delicate parachutes of a dandelion (left).

Scattered by animals

Larger seeds often need the help of animals. Many fruits are brightly colored and tasty to eat. In this way they attract birds and other animals (Picture 3). For example, squirrels and birds carry acorns from oak trees.

You will remember that seeds have a tough coat, so they are not digested, but pass through the animal unaltered, usually surrounded by a ready-made pile of **NUTRITIOUS** manure.

Some fruits do not attract animals and instead "hitch a ride" (Picture 4). These plants mainly grow low to the ground. Each seed has many hooks on its surface that can attach themselves to fur or feathers until they are rubbed or picked off.

Scattered by the oceans

Some seeds, mainly of certain plants that live beside rivers or on the seashore, can float. These seeds can be carried long distances until they reach some far-off shallow. Coconuts (Picture 5) and mangroves are examples.

◄ **(Picture 3)** The bright-red and juicy fruits of the mountain ash (rowan) attract birds.

▶ **(Picture 4)** The sharp hooks of the burr clasp onto unaware travelers.

▼ **(Picture 5)** A coconut washed in on the tide has sprouted and is growing on the beach.

Summary

- Seeds need to be carried from their parent plant.
- Some seeds are carried by the wind.
- Some seeds are carried by animals.
- Some seeds can float on water.

How plants survive

If a plant is to get through its life cycle, it has to have ways of staying alive and getting its seeds to thrive.

All living things survive over time only if they can stay alive long enough to produce at least one offspring to replace each adult.

This is not as easy as it sounds. Many things can prevent a plant from producing seeds or destroy the seeds.

▼ **(Picture 1) This is the life cycle of the poppy. It is typical of many short-lived flowering plants.**

Short life (annual plant)

The poppy is an example of a plant that completes its entire life cycle in one year (Picture 1). It therefore has just one chance of successfully producing a new generation. How does it do this? By producing as many seeds in a year as a long-lived plant may produce in a century. The tiny black seeds that are crammed into the seed pod are shaken out after the seed pod opens, so they are scattered away from the parent plant.

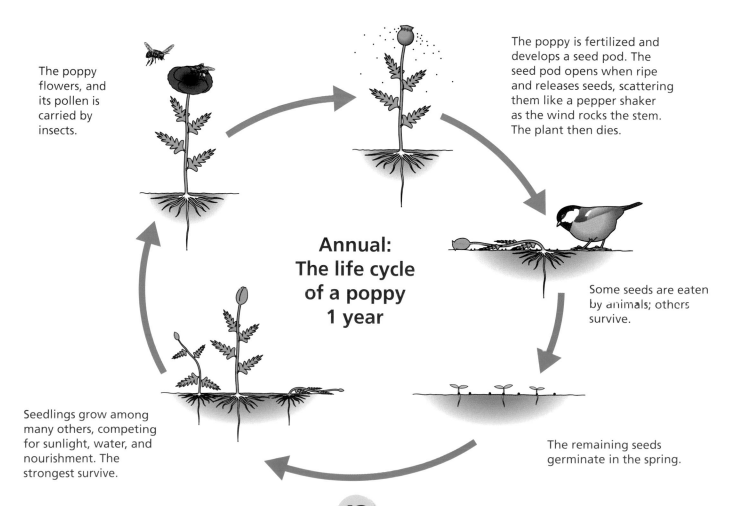

The poppy flowers, and its pollen is carried by insects.

The poppy is fertilized and develops a seed pod. The seed pod opens when ripe and releases seeds, scattering them like a pepper shaker as the wind rocks the stem. The plant then dies.

Annual: The life cycle of a poppy 1 year

Some seeds are eaten by animals; others survive.

Seedlings grow among many others, competing for sunlight, water, and nourishment. The strongest survive.

The remaining seeds germinate in the spring.

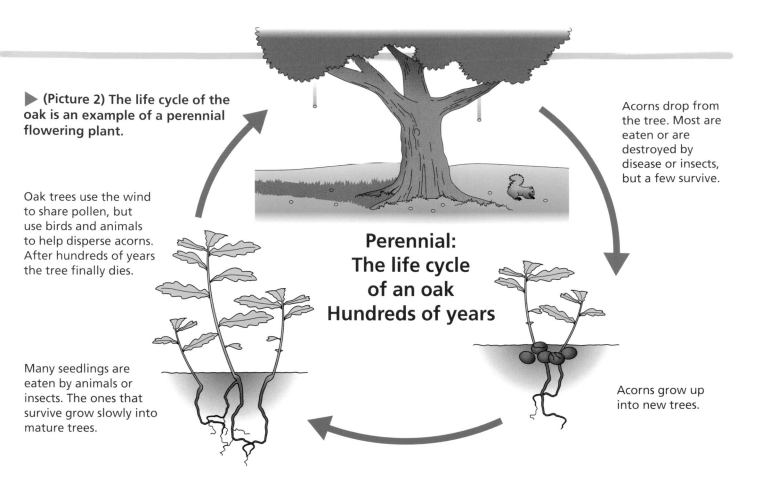

▶ **(Picture 2) The life cycle of the oak is an example of a perennial flowering plant.**

Oak trees use the wind to share pollen, but use birds and animals to help disperse acorns. After hundreds of years the tree finally dies.

Acorns drop from the tree. Most are eaten or are destroyed by disease or insects, but a few survive.

Perennial: The life cycle of an oak Hundreds of years

Many seedlings are eaten by animals or insects. The ones that survive grow slowly into mature trees.

Acorns grow up into new trees.

When the following spring comes, those seeds that have survived will grow swiftly, flowering and setting seed within just a few short weeks.

Long life (perennial plant)

A perennial has a life cycle stretching over many years (Picture 2). An oak tree, for example, produces acorns each year for hundreds of years. What is all this for? Just to make sure that at least one more tree grows up.

The acorns of the oak tree grow best if they can be buried in the ground. Acorns are large, **NUTRITIOUS** seeds that many animals like to eat. Squirrels and other animals carry the acorns away to bury in the ground as a supply of food to be dug up during winter. If only one of them is

not dug up, then a seedling can grow.

But that is not the end of the story. Many seedlings will be eaten by animals like deer. Some will be attacked by caterpillars, and all of their leaves will be eaten away. Even when the few seedlings that survive have grown up, it will be many years before they can produce acorns. In the meanwhile, they may be struck by lightning or suffer some disease.

That is why each mature tree must continue to produce huge numbers of acorns every year.

Summary
• **Plants have many ways of making sure their seeds survive.**
• **Most plants have to produce many seeds to ensure just one survives.**

A new human life begins

Human life depends on sending chemical instructions to new cells.

Humans are much more complicated than plants. But just as with all living things, human life requires the right set of ingredients to make new cells and some instructions (Picture 1). The instructions are chemical packages called **GENES**. They contain the information for making all of the substances needed for life.

Genes

Think of the way genes work as a recipe book that lays down rules for working with ingredients.

There are more than sixty billion cells in the human body, and nearly all of them have their own genetic information. They hold the secrets of how we develop.

Fertilization

Men carry half of the instructions to form new life in special sex cells called **SPERM**, and women carry the other half in special cells called **EGGS**.

A man and a woman have to unite to provide a way for the sperm to reach the eggs (Picture 2).

▼ (Picture 2) The sperm has to travel to the egg. This is easier if it is carrying relatively little "baggage." So it is "slimmed down," mainly containing just chromosomes. Its tail helps it swim to the egg.

The female egg does not travel, and so it keeps most of the original cell material and is larger, containing not just chromosomes, but other essential materials for making new cells.

Sperm cell (half a set of instructions)

New life (complete set of instructions)

Egg cell (half a set of instructions)

▲▼ (Picture 1) When the sperm and egg cells combine, material from both cells mixes together to create a complete set of instructions, or genes, to allow a new life to form.

A gene is a specific piece of information in the form of chemical instructions. Very large numbers of such genes are needed to provide all the instructions for a living thing. Genes are found on structures called chromosomes inside the middle part of the cell, called the nucleus.

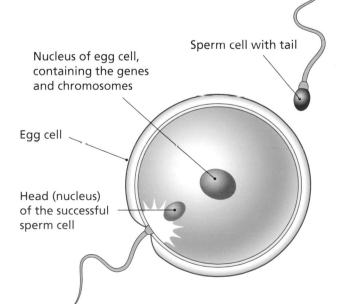
Nucleus of egg cell, containing the genes and chromosomes

Sperm cell with tail

Egg cell

Head (nucleus) of the successful sperm cell

During fertilization the genes from each parent combine to form a complete set of instructions again. The newly fertilized egg can now begin to grow.

Growing

The fertilized egg grows by dividing many, many times (Picture 3).

At first, the growing person, called an embryo, does not look much like a human. But as cells become instructed to specialize in various ways, the growing body becomes much more recognizable.

Thus what begins as a tiny shapeless ball of cells, folds over, stretches, uncurls, and grows limbs (Picture 4). During this process genes instruct cells how to make the properties that will provide for life.

Once a baby is born, the changes do not stop, but continue throughout life. But by birth the fastest changes are finished; and as people get older, the changes occur more and more slowly.

Summary

- Life begins when genes from a man and a woman come together in a fertilized egg.
- The original egg keeps dividing and growing, using the instructions from its genes.

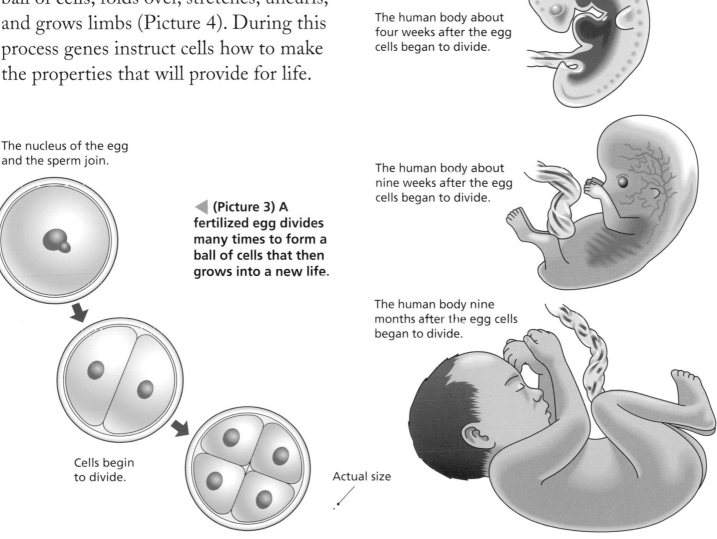

▼ (Picture 4) The early stages of life inside the womb.

Actual size

The human body about four weeks after the egg cells began to divide.

The human body about nine weeks after the egg cells began to divide.

The human body nine months after the egg cells began to divide.

The nucleus of the egg and the sperm join.

◀ (Picture 3) A fertilized egg divides many times to form a ball of cells that then grows into a new life.

Cells begin to divide.

Actual size

Growing older

As people grow older, they change shape. At first they get taller and thinner compared to their height, then later on they get shorter again.

You will notice many changes in your body during your school years. You only have to compare people in a class above you and below you to begin to see some of these changes (Picture 1).

Growing upward

One of the easiest changes to spot is that people grow taller during their school years. Children grow taller very quickly. By your late teens you will already have reached your final height. Your head grows taller, too, so that if you look back at photographs of yourself when you were young, you will see that your face is now narrower than it was.

Changes in height occur at different ages in girls and boys. Girls usually have a spurt of growth when they are about 10 or 11 years old. At this time they may become taller than boys of the same age.

Boys usually have their spurt of growth later, when they are between 13 and 15. It is during this time that they become, on average, taller than girls.

Filling out

You grow in two ways: you first grow taller, then you fill out. If you grow tall but do not fill out at the same rate, you look tall and thin. You are not unhealthy; it's just that filling out will happen later in life for you.

As you fill out, you develop bigger bones and bigger muscles. You can see this in feet shapes and sizes (Picture 2). With bigger muscles you become stronger, so growing up means growing stronger, too.

Girls and boys both weigh about the same when they are 8 years old. Girls then put on more weight than boys and become heavier until about age 14, when boys overtake them again.

Age 11 years
Height 152cm
Weight 54kg

Age 8 years
Height 129cm
Weight 32kg

Age 6 years
Height 113cm
Weight 20kg

◀ **(Picture 1) As people get older, they get taller; they fill out, and they put on weight.**

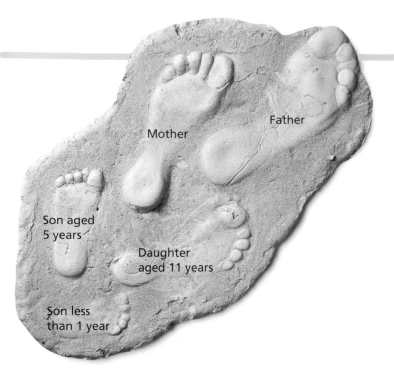

◀ (Picture 2) Feet change shape just like the rest of the body. Here you can see casts of the feet of a family. Notice that the feet get longer compared to their width as the people get older. You may notice other changes in shape, too.

Mother

Father

Son aged 5 years

Daughter aged 11 years

Son less than 1 year

The later years

You are tallest and strongest by your early twenties. Then you may fill out even more. By your sixties you will start to get shorter again as your bones shrink and your muscles become less powerful (Picture 3). This completes your growth cycle.

Growing hair

Hair is one of the last things to grow. Look at your arms, and you will see that they are covered with fine, almost invisible hairs. But if you look at an adult's arm, you will see that the hairs are thicker, longer, and in the case of men, darker.

Summary

- Boys and girls grow at different rates during their lives.
- People grow tall first, then fill out.
- As people get older, they get shorter again.

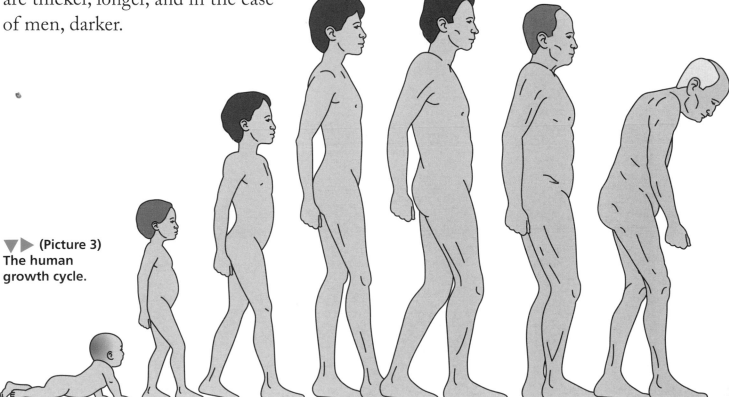

▼▶ (Picture 3)
The human growth cycle.

The life cycle of an insect

Insects do not grow up steadily as people do. Instead, they change shape completely at different stages in their life.

People spend most of their lives as adults. Adults and children also look much the same. Children simply get bigger as they grow up.

But that is not the case with many insects. When you watch a butterfly, for example, you are watching an insect that is coming to the end of its life cycle (Picture 1). It may only have a few weeks, or even days, to live.

Most of the life of an insect is spent in quite a different form. In the case of a butterfly most of its life may be spent as a caterpillar.

Insects vary a lot in their life cycles, so here we will simply look at a butterfly.

The first stage

A butterfly begins as an egg. When the egg hatches, a long, many-legged caterpillar scrambles out. This first stage is called a **LARVA**.

Molting

Insects cannot grow bigger steadily in the same way as we do. That is because they have a hard outer skin that does not stretch.

As a result, an insect has to grow in stages. When an insect is ready to get bigger, it sheds, or **MOLTS**, its old skin.

▶ (Picture 1) The life cycle of a butterfly.

Caterpillars may molt several times.

The new skin is soft and will stretch to the size needed. The insect pumps up its new skin before it hardens, so the hardened skin starts out being too big, and some of the space is filled with air. But as the caterpillar grows, the space is filled. As soon as there is no more room to grow, the caterpillar molts its skin and pumps up a new one.

From pupa to adult

When a larva is fully grown, it begins the dramatic change that will turn it into an adult. Its skin hardens in a case, called a **PUPA**, and inside it develops into an adult.

After some time the hard case splits, and the adult insect struggles out. It is no longer a fat caterpillar with many legs, but a delicate butterfly with folded wings. For a few minutes the butterfly has to let its wings dry, and then it can fly away.

Summary
- The life cycle of many insects is: egg, larva, pupa, and adult.
- In their larval stage insects grow by molting.
- Insects finally change form completely through a stage called a pupa.

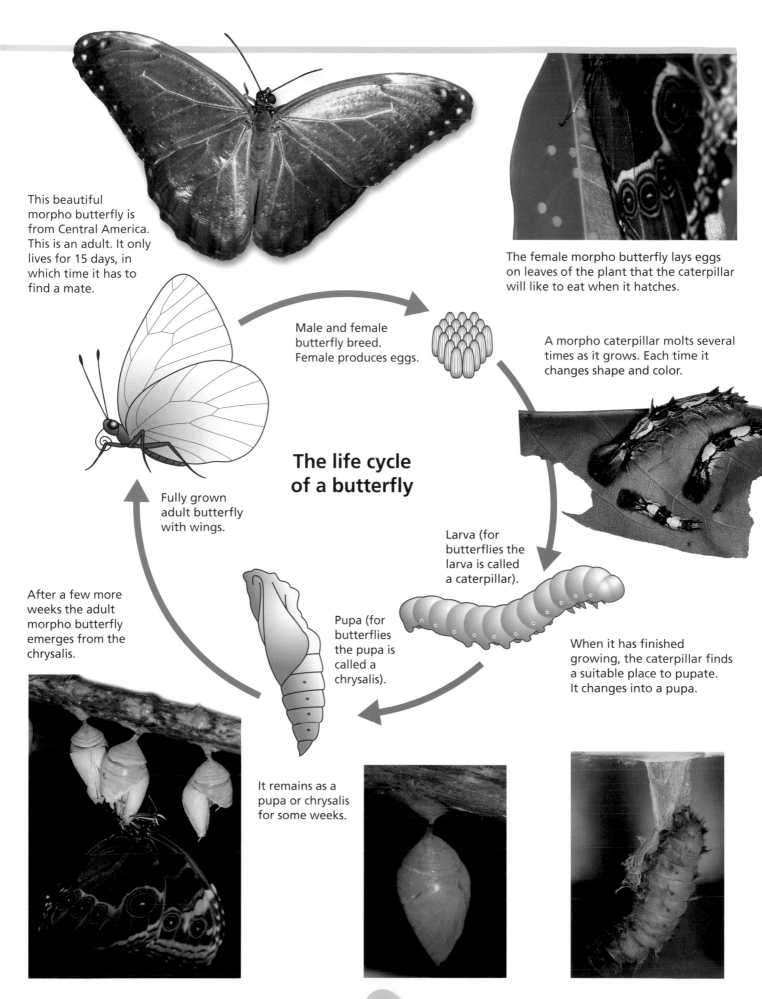

This beautiful morpho butterfly is from Central America. This is an adult. It only lives for 15 days, in which time it has to find a mate.

The female morpho butterfly lays eggs on leaves of the plant that the caterpillar will like to eat when it hatches.

Male and female butterfly breed. Female produces eggs.

A morpho caterpillar molts several times as it grows. Each time it changes shape and color.

The life cycle of a butterfly

Fully grown adult butterfly with wings.

Larva (for butterflies the larva is called a caterpillar).

After a few more weeks the adult morpho butterfly emerges from the chrysalis.

Pupa (for butterflies the pupa is called a chrysalis).

When it has finished growing, the caterpillar finds a suitable place to pupate. It changes into a pupa.

It remains as a pupa or chrysalis for some weeks.

The life cycle of a frog

Frogs live the first part of their lives underwater as tadpoles. Then they lose their gills and begin to breathe air.

Some animals spend the first parts of their lives in water and the later part of their lives mainly on land. One such animal is the frog (Picture 1).

Tadpoles

Frogs begin life as eggs. These eggs are found in clumps called frog spawn. When the eggs hatch, small tadpoles, called larva, emerge.

Frogs live as tadpoles for about three months. During this time they remain completely in water. Tadpoles start life with gills. The gills are used for breathing—taking in oxygen from the water. Tadpoles eat tiny plants called algae that grow on stones in the water. They use rasplike teeth to scrape off the algae. Larger tadpoles, however, become more ferocious and may even eat one another if they get too crowded.

When a tadpole is about two months old, it begins to form legs, first at the back, then at the front. At the same time, its tail starts to disappear.

When the tadpole is three months old, its gills change into lungs, and it has to come to the water surface to breathe.

When the tadpole no longer has a tail, it sheds its skin and becomes a tiny frog.

▼▶ **(Picture 1) The life cycle of a frog.**

These adult frogs are mating. The female may lay hundreds of eggs. As she does so, the male riding on her back fertilizes them.

Frogs

It takes the frog about four years to grow into an adult. Throughout its life on land it feeds on insects instead of plants. It still lives close to water; and when it is ready to breed, the female frog lays her eggs in water so that the tadpoles will hatch underwater.

Summary
- Frogs hatch from eggs as tadpoles.
- Tadpoles live in water and start their lives with gills.
- As a tadpole changes to a frog, it develops legs and lungs.

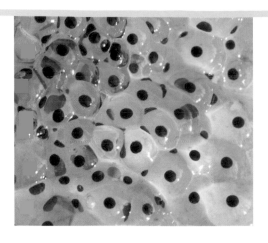

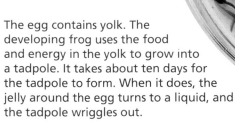

Male and female frogs breed. Females lay masses of eggs—called spawn—in water.

The egg contains yolk. The developing frog uses the food and energy in the yolk to grow into a tadpole. It takes about ten days for the tadpole to form. When it does, the jelly around the egg turns to a liquid, and the tadpole wriggles out.

Fully grown adult frog with lungs, powerful back legs, and no tail.

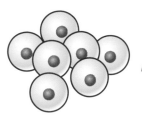

Tadpole larva. The early tadpole breathes through gills.

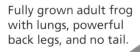

The life cycle of a frog

After about 16 weeks the tadpole moves onto land, and its tail shrinks.

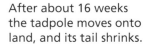

As the tadpole grows and gets older, it grows legs and develops lungs inside its body. It has to come to the surface to breathe.

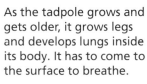

The early stage of the frog is called the tadpole. It is shaped like a fish so it can move easily through the water and has a powerful tail to help it swim. It does not have fins like a fish, which would help it control its movements, so it tends to thrash around in the water. This tadpole is only about 2cm long.

Avoiding extinction

10

Living things only survive over time if they can breed and replace themselves.

All living things have a natural **LIFE SPAN**. At the end of their life span they die. So while they are alive, it is vital that they produce new life that can carry on their line.

However, throughout their lives living things are always in danger. They may not get enough water or food; they may be eaten, have an accident, or die early from disease.

The living things that can cope best with these problems survive, while those that cannot cope become smaller in number and finally all die out. When this happens, they have become **EXTINCT**.

How people cause extinction

Extinctions have been very common in the past, as, for example, the extinction of dinosaurs shows. However, in recent centuries many more **SPECIES** have become extinct than would be due to natural causes. In these cases extinction has been caused by people.

People are one of the most adaptable and successful of all living things. But the more people there are, the more food they need for themselves, and the more they clear the land for farming. As a result, the places other living things need to survive are lost (Picture 1).

The animals that suffer first are those that need large territories or that eat only a small range of foods. Bears and wolves have long been lost from much of Europe. Most large cats, such as tigers and lions, are now threatened, as is the giant panda in China, which feeds mainly on a certain kind of bamboo.

But it is not just the amount of land that gets smaller. Suitable land gets cut off into patches that are far apart. Eventually, the few remaining animals are scattered too far apart

◄ (Picture 1) The Ethiopian wolf is one of the rarest meat-eaters (carnivores) on the planet. There are probably fewer than 500 left, and nearly all of them live in one national park in the highlands of Ethiopia. With continued pressure from people and domesticated herds of animals, the wolf's habitat is being destroyed. Without the help of zoos, it is likely that this species will be extinct before you die.

to find each other to breed. As a result, many wild animals have become extinct.

The purpose of zoos

Zoos were originally collections of animals to amuse the curious. But today zoos play an important part in saving animals from extinction and helping people learn about the importance of animals (Picture 2). Many specialize in the care and breeding of certain animals.

Zoos work together to make breeding programs for their animals. As the population of zoo animals increases, some are released back into their natural environments.

Wilderness areas

Wilderness areas are large pieces of land that are set aside for wildlife. In these natural environments large animals can thrive and not compete with people. Many countries now have wilderness areas, often called national parks. Many more such areas are desperately needed (Picture 3).

WE OCELOTS ARE LUCKY! WHY? BECAUSE YOU HUMANS HAVE MADE it ILLEGAL TO HUNT US FOR OUR FUR!! AND it WOULD TAKE 100 CATS LIKE ME TO MAKE 1 COAT!! NOW is THAT ANY WAY TO TREAT YOUR NATURAL HERITAGE?!! THANKS FOR CHANGING THAT CRAZINESS AND GIVING WE OCELOTS A FUTURE IN THE WILD!!

◀ **(Picture 2)** This sign and animal were photographed in a zoo.

▼ **(Picture 3)** Rain forests contain the greatest diversity of animals and plants in the world. If tropical rain forests continue to be destroyed at the current rate, it is estimated that more than a million species of insect alone will become extinct in the next 30 to 50 years.

Summary

- Living things depend on the survival of their natural environments to complete their life cycles.
- If the amount of wilderness shrinks or becomes split up, animals can become extinct.
- Animals can best be saved from extinction by protecting the wilderness.

Index

Science Matters!

Grolier Educational

First published in the United States in 2003 by Grolier Educational, Sherman Turnpike, Danbury, CT 06816

Copyright © 2003
Atlantic Europe Publishing Company Ltd.

All rights reserved. No part of this publication may be reproduced, stored in a retrieval system, or transmitted in any form or by any means— electronic, mechanical, photocopying, recording, or otherwise—without prior permission of the publisher.

This product is manufactured from sustainable managed forests. For every tree cut down at least one more is planted.

Author
Brian Knapp, BSc, PhD

Educational Consultant
Peter Riley, BSc, C Biol, MI Biol, PGCE

Art Director
Duncan McCrae, BSc

Senior Designer
Adele Humphries, BA, PGCE

Editor
Lisa Magloff, BA

Illustrations
David Woodroffe

Designed and produced by
Earthscape Editions

Reproduced in Malaysia by
Global Color

Printed in Hong Kong by
Wing King Tong Company Ltd

Picture credits
All photographs are from the Earthscape Editions photolibrary.

Library of Congress Cataloging-in-Publication Data
Knapp, Dr. Brian J.
    Science Matters! / [Dr. Brian J. Knapp].
      p. cm.
    Includes index.
    Summary: Presents information on a wide variety of topics in basic biology, chemistry, and physics.
    Contents: v. 1. Food, teeth, and eating—v. 2. Helping plants grow well—v. 3. Properties of materials—v. 4. Rocks and soils—v. 5. Springs and magnets—v. 6. Light and shadows—v. 7. Moving and growing—v. 8. Habitats—v. 9. Keeping warm and cool—v. 10. Solids and liquids—v. 11. Friction—v. 12. Simple electricity—v. 13. Keeping healthy—v. 14. Life cycles—v. 15. Gases around us—v. 16. Changing from solids to liquids to gases—v. 17. Earth and beyond—v. 18. Changing sounds—v. 19. Adapting and surviving—v. 20. Microbes—v. 21. Dissolving—v. 22. Changing materials—v. 23. Forces in action—v. 24. How we see things—v. 25. Changing circuits.
    ISBN 0-7172-5834-3 (set)—ISBN 0-7172-5835-1 (v. 1)—ISBN 0-7172-5836-X (v. 2)—ISBN 0-7172-5837-8 (v. 3)—ISBN 0-7172-5838-6 (v. 4)—ISBN 0-7172-5839-4 (v. 5)—ISBN 0-7172-5840-8 (v. 6)—ISBN 0-7172-5841-6 (v. 7)—ISBN 0-7172-5842-4 (v. 8)—ISBN 0-7172-5843-2 (v. 9)—ISBN 0-7172-5844-0 (v. 10)—ISBN 0-7172-5845-9 (v. 11)—ISBN 0-7172-5846-7 (v. 12)—ISBN 0-7172-5847-5 (v. 13)—ISBN 0-7172-5848-3 (v. 14)—ISBN 0-7172-5849-1 (v. 15)—ISBN 0-7172-5850-5 (v. 16)—ISBN 0-7172-5851-3 (v. 17)—ISBN 0-7172-5852-1 (v. 18)—ISBN 0-7172-5853-X (v. 19)—ISBN 0-7172-5854-8 (v. 20)—ISBN 0-7172-5855-6 (v. 21)—ISBN 0-7172-5856-4 (v. 22)—ISBN 0-7172-5857-2 (v. 23)—ISBN 0-7172-5858-0 (v. 24)—ISBN 0-7172-5859-9 (v. 25)
    1. Science—Juvenile literature. [1. Science.] I. Title.

Q163.K48 2002
500—dc21

2002017302